MW01143225

THE

MONEY GAME

BY JESSEE WARREN

www.moneyitsagame.com
Information:

(909) 465-9733
E-mail:
info@moneyitsagame.com

WARREN PUBLISHING COMPANY
P. O. Box 146
Pomona, CA 91769

CONTENTS

*THE FUTURE REALLY CAN BE BRIGHTER, TRY
IT, IT WORKED FOR ME...*

INTRODUCTION

THE MONEY GAME IS THE ONLY GAME IN TOWN. SINCE YOU HAVE NO CHOICE BUT TO PLAY, THE ONLY INTELLIGENT THING TO DO IS TO LEARN THE RULES AND PLAY TO WIN!

Losing means spending your life in angry frustration, in a state of financial insecurity and in despair.

If you have no choice but to play the game, and if it is so essential that you win, why weren't you taught how to play this game successfully in school?

I really do not know. There is an educational void in our country. We are spending millions of dollars teaching both young people and adults to earn dollars; yet we are not teaching them what to do with these dollars to maximize their purchasing power once those dollars have been earned. I believe we are making a tragic mistake, a substantial portion of our population spend most of their income on basic essentials.

Somewhere during the beginning of time or later on, emerged the sinister concept of "money is the root of all evil." This is not true. It is the love for and misuse of money that brings corruption and human suffering. The proper use of money provides the necessary food for the family; it helps build hospitals; it help build churches in which to worship; it provides shelter from the cold and heat, money in itself is nothing, but its the love of money that causes one to do things that he or she would not ordinary do. Money is good.

Money, is not merely money, it is not just something you spend for what you want. It is the reward for your work, the product of a job well done, a helper, a servant that will work for you. It is a trip to the islands, a life saver in emergencies, for you or members of the family, or friends. Money is the product of your labor, or it can be if you manage it properly.

Just as people grow with time and experience, and become bigger, better and more useful persons, money can grow and become a useful partner. The two of you working together as one.

Money is a beginning in itself, and a means to all sorts of beginnings.

I feel I should warn you now that applying the information contained in this book will not give you instant wealth. If I knew how to do that, as committed as I am to helping others become financially independent, do you really think I would be willing to sell my secret for such a small sum as the price of a book.

I am convinced that if you have a reasonable amount of time, the ability and willingness to earn an average wage, the discipline to save a small portion of your earnings, and the intelligence to apply the principles discussed in this book, you can become financially independent. Attainment of this desir-able state does not require brilliance or luck. It requires discipline, agility, and the ability and willingness to make your dollars work for you as hard as you had to work for it.

This book is the result of many years of financial and investment experiences, that started with Ford Motor Company, Bank of America, Department of Justice, owning several properties and my financial consulting firm.

The goal of this book is to present a number of concepts and practices that if applied properly can lead to getting the most out of your hard earned dollars. We, as americans consumer, out of sheer carelessness waste so much of our hard earned income until its simply mine boggling. We see it, we want it, we purchase it, not really considering the cost, future cost, what impact it will have on our finances or how we are going to pay for it. In our world of plastic (the credit card) most consumers are not aware of the ultimate financial consequences of using the credit unwisely or maybe we just do not care.

REMEMBER THE MONEY RULE....WE ALL LIVE BY THE MONEY RULE, WHOEVER HAS THE MONEY MAKE THE RULE....

PLANNING YOUR PERSONAL
FINANCIAL FUTURE

$$
$$
$$

$ $ $ $ $ THE MONEY GAME $ $ $ $ $

                         $$$$$$$$$$$$$$$
$$$
$$$$$$$$$$$$$$$
                         $$$$$$$$$$$$$$$
$$$
$$$$$$$$$$$$$$$

MONEY MATTERS

When it comes to money most of us hear
two voices.

One cautions us to save for future goals
and the other tempts us to buy what we
want right now.

Well, the truth is, most of us cannot have everything, at least not all at once. On the other hand, we do not have to give up everything we enjoy to meet our future goals. Whatever your goals may be, they can come true if you stop dreaming and start doing. The secret to getting what you want now and in the future is good planning.

Sometimes we are torn between dreams for the future and those we want to come true now. When we dream about a goal that is important to us, we tell ourselves, "you can do it if you put your mind to it." Then the other voice might tell us that we work hard and deserve some pleasure now, such as eating out, buying new clothes, taking a weekend trip, or going to a concert.

Whether or not we fulfill our dreams depends on the choices we make every day. Even if you feel you are living from paycheck to paycheck, you can make choices that allow you to enjoy life today and make the most of your money in the future.

MOST PEOPLE DO NOT PLAN TO FAIL -- THEY FAIL TO PLAN

Have you ever reached into your wallet for a $20 bill, only to find just a five and some ones? Where did that $20 go? You just got it from the ATM yesterday, and it is already gone. So you start adding it up. Lunch yesterday, newspapers, pastry, and coffee -- $7.00. We can spend $20 without even realizing it. And all those $20 bills that get away can really add up.

When you do not have a spending plan, it is a safe bet those $20 bills will disappear, and you will not get where you want to go.

PAY YOURSELF FIRST, BEFORE YOU PAY ANYONE ELSE

What can you do to make sure you get what you really want? Ask yourself this question every time you get paid -- How am I going to use this paycheck to reach my goal?

After you ask this question, you may realize one or two things -- You have not been spending anything to reach your goal, or you have not been spending enough to reach your goal. If, either is true, each time you get that paycheck, spend some money on your goal before you spend it on anything else. In other words, pay yourself, before you pay anyone else.

3

Successful financial planning requires attention to a variety of areas, including:

* Creating an emergency fund: goal 6 months of expenses

* Setting financial objectives and planning ahead to meet them

* Organizing your personal records: receipts, pictures, serial numbers, etc.

* Managing your debt effectively and bringing your spending under control: How much debt do you owe?

* Saving 5% regularly short-term and investing long-term

* Accumulating an investment portfolio that meets your lifetime needs

* Minimizing your taxes

* Planning to retire when you want to, how you want to, and without fear of running out of money during your retirement years

Do not be surprised if you find the financial planning process rather overwhelming at first. There is a lot to do,

even if your finances are already in
pretty good order. But, if you begin to
do one thing, you will find that you can
improve your personal financial status.
Begin with paying yourself first!

It is not such a burden, in fact,
it will be enjoyable to watch your
investments grow, to finally get your
debt and spending under control and enjoy
a long and financially fruitful life.

COMMITTED AND FOCUSED

As you go after your goals, your most valuable tool is your commitment. The key is to stay focused on your "goal" even when you have to cope with external problems and internal sabotage. Some useful skills will help you stay motivated when attacked by obstacles of every day life.

1. **Be confident,** stop dwelling on what you might not be able to do. See yourself doing it. Relax and give it your all.

2. **Recognize,** do not exaggerate, your shortcomings. Assess your weaknesses honestly, then apply a little more eagerness to deal with them. Attend a seminar to help you overcome an inadquacy or read a self-improvement book.

3. **Do not give up** -- "The road to success is paved with failures" and "He who will not be denied will find a way" and "Winners are ordinary people with extraordinary determination" are truisms. Only

6

by overcoming difficulties can you
become a winner. Expect obstacles
and learn from setbacks. Do not
consider yourself a failure, if
fail at something. **Tip**: If you
make your goals reasonable and
manageable, you are more likely to
reach them.

4. *Remember pleasant things*: Make a
list of your accomplishments and
repeat them to yourself every day
while you are driving, or getting
ready for work, and so on. Think
of your mind as a computer with a
video monitor. Project images of
yourself having accomplished your
goals. Then program in positive
information about yourself.

5. *Flexibility is the key*: Choose
and explore a wide variety of
approaches to your goals. If new
developments or changed circumstances demand it, drop an
unworkable approach and take
up another. Learn to shift
gears, change perspectives,
modify approaches, and adapt
quickly to new requirements.
"BOMBARD" your goals with a
variety of alternative solutions.

6. *Pay attention*: Listen with an
open mind to other people's
suggestions, ideas, and advise.
Sometimes discussing your plans

or problems with others who are unfamiliar with your goals or problems can give you a new slant. Often people have a fresh point of view and can make you aware of approaches you may have overlooked.

7. *Risk is part of the money game*: Most successful people possess an adventurous spirit. Be willing to leap into the unknown and give up the routines and habits that only appear to make the future secure and predictable but in fact sentence you to stagnation.

8. *Develop an I can attitude*: If you occasionally feel stumped or discouraged, remind yourself of a past success. Spend a fair amount of time recalling the situation in vivid detail. You will recapture a sense of confidence. You will also discover that you can do whatever is necessary and that the achievement of your goals is well within your power.

```
==========================================
         3 3 3 3 3 3 3 3
==========================================
```

PLANNING

AFFORD WHAT YOU WANT, WHEN YOU WANT IT

The one thing we all share in common is our desire to achieve financial security. For most people, financial security means financial independence, the ability to meet all foreseeable financial needs from their own resources. In other words, financial security means being able to afford what you want when you want it or to retire, whether one chooses to retire or not. Everyone wants to be financially independent. We all want the security of being able to cope with whatever financial demands we might encounter.

You do not have to be lucky to achieve financial security. You do have to work at it, and the earlier you begin, the easier it will be to achieve.

KEYS TO ACHIEVING FINANCIAL SECURITY

Formulate objectives. You cannot get there from here unless you establish some important personal financial planning objectives.

Never give up control over your money. Do not let other people tell you what to do with your money. You are your own best financial planner.

Create a nest egg. There is nothing like money in the bank to give you financial peace of mind. Kick the spending habit, and get hooked on saving regularly.

Cope with major life events. Life deals each of us a variety of cards, some are good, and some are not so good. Preparing for the unexpected helps minimize financial disruptions, the key is good planning.

Invest wisely. Learning about how to invest and putting your knowledge to work is one of the most important ingredients to your financial security.

Learn to live beneath your means. The only way to accumulate the investments necessary to achieve financial security is to spend less than you earn, and the only way to spend less than you earn is to live beneath your means.

Use credit wisely. Credit can be useful in achieving financial security, or it can destroy your financial security. It all depends on how you use it.

Take the time to attend to your finances. The time you spend to work on your personal finances is always time well spent. No one is going to take more interest in your financial/personal affairs than you. It's like putting money in the bank.

Invest in your career. Devote the time necessary to improve your skills and advance in your career. Your career is your most important income-producing investment.

Participate in retirement plans. Maximize your participation in tax-advantaged retirement plans to help assure a comfortable retirement.

Set the record straight. Organize your records and prepare personal financial statements to get a better handle on your finances.

You are responsible for achieving financial security. It is up to you to take the actions necessary to achieve financial independence. YOU CAN DO IT....

EVALUATE "YOUR" PAST
(Is it really depressing?)

Your Personal
Financial Planner

Successful personal financial planning requires attention to distinct areas including, but by no means limited to the following: getting organized, accumulating and protecting your investments, and planning for later in life.

Never Underestimate
the Value of COMMON SENSE

Personal financial planning really is not that complicated. All it takes is some discipline, a little time, and the willingness to either be your own financial planner or to make sure your financial planning advisor(s) are acting in your best interest.

If successful financial planning can be boiled down to two words, they are common sense. If you think back on the dumb things you have done with your money in the past, and no one is immune to doing dumb things with their money, you

will no doubt find that your money
calamities were caused by lapses of
common sense on your part.

Learn How to
Communicate About Matters of Finance

In an age when business, economics,
and household budgets dominate the news
as well as everyday conversation, it is
amazing how little most of us truly know
about basic financial planning.

* Parents should talk with your
  children to educate them about
  your financial errors and
  successes.

* Talk to friends and other
  associates that possess a
  knowledge of personal finance and
  investing.

* Use the public library for
  financial planning and investment information.

* Don't make talking about money
  such a big issue. We have all
  made more mistakes than we care
  to admit. The more knowledge we
  acquire while growing up, the
  better prepared we will be to
  cope with finances each day of
  our adult life. The problem is,

13

we are not acquiring the knowledge to prepare us for the
obstacles that lie ahead as we
venture into the world of high
tech finance and investment
trends.

* Local community colleges offer
  financial planning courses,
  enroll in a course.

SETTING UP PRIORITIES

Once you cut back on your spending,
you will need to decide what to do with
the extra money you free up. Here are
some suggestions to consider:

* Build an emergency cash reserve
  fund. Most financial planners
  recommend you have at least
  3 months salary in easily accessible investments to cover
  unexpected expenses.

* Pay off high-interest debt, such
  as credit cards and other loans.
  Use the money you save in
  interest to build your savings.

* Focus on long-term needs, such as
  adequate retirement income.
  Consider increasing your contri-
  bution to your company investment
  plan that provides matching
  funds. Or invest in other funds

that do not pose a very high risk
factor.

* Focus on short-term goals such as
  a vacation, buying a house, or
  college education for the kids.

QUICK STATEMENT OF PERSONAL
ASSETS AND LIABILITIES

===
Personal Assets
===

CASH $_____

INVESTMENTS (stocks,MMA,CD,etc.)   _____

REAL ESTATE (residence)   _____

REAL ESTATE (other)   _____

RETIREMENT PLANS   _____

OTHER ASSETS   _____

_____   _____

_____   _____

_____   _____

_____   _____

Total Assets $_____

16

==
Personal Liabilities
==

CREDIT CARDS AND CHARGE
ACCOUNTS $_____

AUTO LOANS   _____

MORTGAGES   _____

OTHER BANK LOANS   _____

OTHER LIABILITIES   _____

_____   _____

_____   _____

_____   _____

_____   _____

Total Liabilities $_____

**Total Net Worth (Assets less
Liabilities)** $_____

17

```
===========================================
        5 5 5 5 5 5 5 5
===========================================
```

A PERSONAL BUDGET
(It can be fun)

Budgeting, for individuals and families, is one of the most important steps to personal financial security. The purposes of budgeting are:

* TO SEE WHERE YOUR MONEY IS GOING

* TO DEFINE POSSIBLE PROBLEMS IN SPENDING PATTERNS

* TO IDENTIFY OPPORTUNITIES TO OVERCOME THE PROBLEMS

* TO HELP YOU PLAN REALISTICALLY TO BALANCE YOUR SPENDING WITH YOUR INCOME

A BUDGET CAN HELP YOU REACH YOUR FINANCIAL GOALS

Most people think of budgeting as a punitive task rather than as a positive financial planning step. Nearly all of us have areas in our personal finances where we routinely overspend, or at least do not use our resources as prudently as we might. A budget can help you spot patterns of overspending so that you will not repeat them.

Knowing the amount of income you can reasonably expect to earn and how that income will be spent can go a long way in preventing unforeseen financial problems. How? By knowing what your expenses are, you will be less tempted to overspend. (That is the theory, anyway.) A sensible, practical budget can instill a much needed degree of discipline into your financial affairs. It can also help you devise a plan to reduce debt and increase savings.

PREPARE A PERSONAL BUDGET

Cash Receipts	Projection (One Month)
1. Gross Salary	$_____
2. Interest	_____
3. Dividends	_____
4. Bonuses	_____
5. Alimony/Child Support	_____
6. Dist. from Partnership	_____
7. Business Income	_____
8. Trust Distribution	_____
9. Social Security	_____
10. Gifts	_____
11. Investments	_____
12. Other	
*_____	_____
*_____	_____
13. Total Cash Receipts	$____

	Cash Disbursements	Projection (One Month)
1.	Rent/Mortgage	$1510.00
2.	Food	43
3.	Household Maintenance	105.00
4.	Utilities and Phone	270.00
5.	Clothing *R-May - Sears - etc?*	100.00
6.	Personal Care	_____
7.	Medical and Dental Care	20.00
8.	Automobile/transportation	0
9.	Child Care Expenses	0
10.	Entertainment *wkd*	160.00
11.	Vacation(s)	_____
12.	Gifts	_____
13.	Contributions	_____
14.	Insurances	_____
15.	Miscellaneous out-of-pocket	_____
16.	Home Improvements	_____
17.	Real-Estate Taxes	_____

18. Loan Payments   526.00

19. Credit Card Payments   800.00

20. Tuition/Educational Expenses   _____

21. Business/Professional Expenses   _____

22. Savings/Investments   _____

23. Income taxes and Soc. Sec. Taxes____

24. Other

    *_____   _____

    *_____   _____

    *_____   _____

    *_____   _____

    *_____   _____

25. Total Cash Disbursements $_____

Excess Cash (Short Fall) $_____
(Subtract Total Cash
Disbursements from Total
Cash Receipts)

22

```
==========================================
            6 6 6 6 6 6 6 6
==========================================
```

TRACK YOUR SPENDING FOR ONE MONTH...
JUST TRY!

Financial statements are a necessary
part of planning your personal financial
future, just as they are for a business.

In fact, your personal financial
life is very similar to that of a business. Like a business, you have assets,
liabilities, income, and expenses.

PREPARING A STATEMENT
OF PERSONAL ASSETS AND LIABILITIES

A Statement of Personal Assets and
Liabilities is an excellent way to gauge
your progress toward achieving financial
security. It's a snapshot of what you
OWN and what you OWE. The principle
behind preparing this statement is
simplicity itself: Add up your assets,
then add up your liabilities. By sub-
tracting liabilities from assets, you
will end up with your NET WORTH. If on
the other hand, your liabilities exceed
your assets, you have a "DEFICIT" net
worth.

STATEMENT OF PERSONAL ASSETS AND LIABILITIES

This worksheet can be used to summarize your assets and liabilities in detail. A column is included so that you can periodically monitor your progress. This worksheet should be prepared at least every 6 months or more frequently, if needed.

TODAY'S DATE _____

ASSETS

1. Cash $_____

2. Money-Market and acct.   _____

3. Fixed Income Investments
   * Savings accounts   _____

   * CDs   _____

   * Government Sec.   _____

   * Corporate Bonds   _____

   * Municipal Bonds   _____

   * Other Fixed income
     investments   _____

24

4. Stock Investments
   * Common Stock _____

   * Stock Mutual Funds _____

   * Other Stock
     Investments _____

5. Real Estate Investments
   * Undeveloped Land _____

   * Directly Owned _____

   * Income-Producing _____

   * Other Real Estate _____

6. Ownership Interest
   In Private Business _____

7. Cash Value of Life
   Insurance Policies _____

8. Retirement-Oriented
   Assets _____

   * Individual Retirement
     Accounts (IRAs) _____

   * Keogh/Pension Plans _____

   * Employee Thrift/Stock
     Purchase Plans _____

   * Other Retirement
     Assets _____

9. Personal Assets
    * Pers. Residence(s)   _____

    * Automobile(s)   _____

    * Jewelry   _____

    * Personal Property   _____

10. Other assets

    *_____   _____

    *_____   _____

    *_____   _____

    *_____   _____

11. **Total Assets** $_____

LIABILITIES

1. Credit/Charge Cards $_____

2. Income Tax Payable _____

3. Misc. Accounts Payable _____

4. Bank Loans _____

5. Policy Loans on Life Ins. _____

6. Automobile Loans _____

7. Student Loans _____

8. Mortgage on Residence _____

9. Mortgage on Investment
   Real Estate _____

10. Other Liabilities

    *_____ _____

    *_____ _____

    *_____ _____

11. **Total Liabilities** $_____

    NET WORTH $_____
    (Total Assets less
    Total Liabilities)

27

Note: Assets should be listed at their current market value. Be realistic in valuing those assets that require an estimated market value, such as home and personal property.

YOUR SPENDING ORGANIZER

1. Each day for one month, keep a record of all the money you spend. Save your canceled checks, credit card receipts, and ATM receipts. Jot down what you spend in cash.

2. At the end of the month, pull out all your records and enter each expense in the appropriate spending category on the worksheet. Here is a description of each category:

Housing: mortgage, rent, utilities, repairs

Child Care: babysitting, day care, after school programs

Food: groceries, restaurant, fast food, snacks, lunch

Health Care: medical, dental, and vision not covered under a plan

Transportation: repairs, maintenance, gas, parking, public transportation cost

28

Insurance: premiums on autos, home-owner's and renter's

Clothes: clothing, shoes, accessories, dry cleaning

Personal: entertainment, gifts, hobbies, etc.

Work Related: work expenses/costs not reimbursed by your employer

Investment Related: MMA, CD, IRA, savings, stocks, mutal funds, and others

Others: anything else you purchase or pay for services, including payments on debts.

A MONTHLY EXPENSE SUMMARY

ITEMS:

	Housing	Child Care	Hlth Care	Food	Trans	Ins
DAY						
1	$_____	$_____	$____	$____	$____	$____
2	$_____	$_____	$____	$____	$____	$____
3	$_____	$_____	$____	$____	$____	$____
4	$_____	$_____	$____	$____	$____	$____
5	$_____	$_____	$____	$____	$____	$____
6	$_____	$_____	$____	$____	$____	$____
7	$_____	$_____	$____	$____	$____	$____
8	$_____	$_____	$____	$____	$____	$____
9	$_____	$_____	$____	$____	$____	$____
10	$_____	$_____	$____	$____	$____	$____
TOTAL	$_____	$_____	$____	$____	$____	$____

30

ITEMS:
         Work
         Related   Clothes   Personal   Others

DAY

1	$_____	$_____	$_____	$_____	$_____	$_____
2	$_____	$_____	$_____	$_____	$_____	$_____
3	$_____	$_____	$_____	$_____	$_____	$_____
4	$_____	$_____	$_____	$_____	$_____	$_____
5	$_____	$_____	$_____	$_____	$_____	$_____
6	$_____	$_____	$_____	$_____	$_____	$_____
7	$_____	$_____	$_____	$_____	$_____	$_____
8	$_____	$_____	$_____	$_____	$_____	$_____
9	$_____	$_____	$_____	$_____	$_____	$_____
10	$_____	$_____	$_____	$_____	$_____	$_____
TOTAL	$_____	$_____	$_____	$_____	$_____	$_____

The example above is for 10 days, you
should prepare your spending expense
organizer for one month.

YOUR SPENDING PLAN

Use the following worksheet to periodically figure out how you can cut back on your expenses and decide how you will use the money you free up to help you reach your goal.

Look at the monthly expenses you listed on worksheet #1. Can you cut back on your spending in any categories to free up extra money?

For example, cutting back on food cost by eating out less or purchasing less junk food, stop wasting utilities or implement ride sharing or use public transportation to work. Write your ideas down and your estimates of how much you can save next to each applicable expense category. Then total your estimated savings.

Category	Changes	Estimated Monthly Savings
Housing	_____	_____
	_____	_____
	_____	_____
Child Care	_____	_____
Food	_____	_____
Health Care	_____	_____
Transportation	_____	_____
Insurance	_____	_____
Work Related	_____	_____
Investment Related	_____	_____
Clothes	_____	_____
Personal	_____	_____
Other	_____	_____
	_____	_____
	_____	_____
Total Monthly Savings		$_____

Now that you have taken a closer look at your spending habits, your priorities may have changed. Rethink which goals are most important to you, and record them below. Then, determine how much of the extra money you will put into your savings.

GOALS	AMOUNT TO SAVE EACH MONTH
1._____	
_____	
_____	$_____
2._____	
_____	
_____	$_____
3._____	
_____	
_____	$_____

```
=========================================
           7 7 7 7 7 7 7
=========================================
```

SPENDING LESS THAN YOU EARN...
STOP CHEATING YOURSELF

Living beneath your means is the
only route to enjoy a secure confort-
able standard of living throughout your
working and retirement years. Living
beneath your means is not a suggestion.

It is imperative -- a must do.
Spend less than you earn. Of course,
most of us have heard this before from
parents, friends, financial advisors, and
other individuals. But who listened?
Not too many people do. All you have to
do is look at where your spending habits
have landed you. If you are like most
people, you have simply ended up repeat-
ing financial mistakes rather than doing
what you know you must to live beneath
your means.

===
THE SINGLE MOST IMPORTANT KEY TO
ACHIEVING FINANCIAL SECURITY:
LIVING BENEATH YOUR MEANS
===

Cutting back on expenses, increasing your savings, adding to your investments, these are things many of us are not accustomed to doing. We are too busy getting what we want when we want it to concern ourselves with such fundamentals as actually owning what we have. The problem is that without steadily increasing your savings and investments, you are literally living on borrowed time. Be assured that a financial crisis will happen, it is just a matter of time. If you do not own the home you live in, the car you drive, or the furniture you sit on, it is no wonder that when the first minor financial problem hits, you do not have the funds to pull you through it.

The fact is that Americans as a culture, a culture of conspicuous consumption, is not the land of the free. It is rather the land of the indebted. It is about time you change your ridiculous spending habits, develop some sound saving habits, and learn to invest regularly and wisely so you can share in a piece of the American dream and not live a debtor's nightmare.

SPEND LESS AND ENJOY LIFE MORE...

* *YOU WILL* no longer have to worry
  about living from paycheck to
  paycheck, wondering and worrying
  about how to meet monthly
  obligations.

* *YOU WILL* no longer have to worry
  about losing everything if you are
  laid off from work or suffer a pay
  cut.

* *YOU WILL* no longer feel compelled
  to keep up with the Joneses, plus
  that concept has never been a good
  one. Live your own life the way
  you want and do not let someone
  else dictate what, when, or how
  you do things.

* *YOU WILL* no longer have to worry
  whether or not you will be able to
  afford your children's tuition or
  have money for those emergencies.

HOW TO LIVE BENEATH YOUR MEANS

To succeed, you have to continually look for ways, both small and large, to cut your expenses. You may think you cannot possibly make your budget any leaner -- you are wrong. Many ways exist for you to cut small amounts off both recurring and annual expenses. While some of the savings may individually seem marginal, in total they will be significant. Unfortantly, people who do not get into the habit of living beneath their means and saving regularly will never achieve financial security.

Remember, saving does not mean having to live like a miser. As your savings grow and your net worth increases, even savers can indulge in luxuries.

BE SELF-SUFFICIENT

When it comes to taking control of our financial lives, many of us have lost the take control drive. But you cannot rely on others to provide sufficient resources to achieve financial security for you. You must do most of it on your very own. Here are some ways:

* THE ONLY WAY TO GET MONEY TO
  INVEST IS TO SAVE REGULARLY

* THE ONLY WAY TO SAVE REGULARLY IS,
  TO SPEND LESS THAN YOU EARN

* THE ONLY WAY TO SPEND LESS THAN
  YOU EARN IS TO LIVE BENEATH YOUR
  MEANS

* IF YOU DO NOT GET INTO THE HABIT
  OF LIVING BENEATH YOUR MEANS, YOU
  WILL NEVER SAVE ENOUGH MONEY TO
  INVEST AND YOU WILL CONTINUE TO
  LIVE FROM PAYCHECK TO PAYCHECK.

DEVELOP A COST-CUTTING PLAN

Cutting expenses is never as difficult as you may think. Like dieting, it is the thought of having to cut back that keep you hungering for more, even when you are not hungry.

EXAMPLE:

Mary and John Doe, like many other couples have not been able to save much. They are now really concerned about their financial future, but feel there is no way they can afford to save. Now, they have come up with the following money-saving ideas:

Weekly Savings for Two

Carry lunch to work $35

Less snacks........................$15

Don't eat out more than once a week..$25

Ride Share to work..................$15

Don't buy lottery tickets...........$10

Other:
   Pocket change................$10
   _____...........
   _____...........

Estimated weekly savings............$110

If they stick to this plan, the Doe's can begin saving without a great deal of suffering. While $110 per week in savings may not sound like a lot, it sure adds up over the months. You will average saving $440 per month (based on 4 weeks) or $5,720 per year.

===
8 8 8 8 8 8 8 8
===

PUTTING YOUR RECORDS IN ORDER

Just suppose that your doctor tells you that you need to have major surgery within the next week and the operation will be followed by a lengthy period of recuperation. Will your personal records be organized well enough to allow your spouse or friend to take charge of your financial affairs on short notice? For many people, the answer is no. As modern life grows more and more complicated, we accumulate a greater number of personal financial documents. Yet too many of us never get around to putting records in order. That is a big mistake. And the problems do not simply involve the possibility that you may be out of commission for a while. Poor record-keeping ends up complicating your financial life and may cost you money.

THE VALUE OF GOOD RECORD-KEEPING

Good record-keeping is valuable for at least two reasons.

First, by making your financial documents easily accessible, you will save time. Admittedly, setting up a recordkeeping system will take time, especially if your records are extremely unorganized. Once the system is up and running, you will no longer have to spend hours looking for a canceled check to prove a disputed bill. Nor will you have to go through innumerable drawers in order to find a receipt.

Second, the process of organizing your records and documents is an excellent way to reacquaint yourself with some of the more neglected areas of your personal financial planning. In organizing your legal documents, for instance, you might find that neither you nor your spouse ever updated your power of attorney, even though you each assumed that the other had done so. Organizing your records will allow you to find out where you stand, which is essential to planning for the future.

SMART MONEY MOVE

SAVE TIME AND MONEY BY ORGANIZING AND MAINTAINING A SIMPLE

PERSONAL RECORD-KEEPING SYSTEM

43

```
=========================================
            9 9 9 9 9 9 9 9
=========================================
```

SETTING FINANCIAL GOALS

I know, goals can be boring, it requires you to think about the past, the present and the future. But you need to get pumped up about them. If you handle this one right, much of the rest of your financial life will fall neatly into place.

One of the key steps in financial planning, probably the most important is determining your goals. When I begin to work with a new client, we talk about this for a long time. We have a freewheeling discussion that last for an extended period of time, before we get down to what the client really wants. That's how out of touch most of us are with our basic desire and deepest goal. They are there: it is just a matter of finding them. Do not stop digging until you are certain about what you want from life and how you plan on acquiring it.

Once you know where you are going, the next step is to decide how to get there.

A balanced, flexible plan allows you to accumulate wealth for tomorrow without sacrificing the money you need for today. You must be patient, however, in accumulating that wealth. Like everyone else, we must crawl before we can walk and walk before we can run. By investing wisely, you will eventually get to the point where you do not need to delay necessary purchases in order to assure your future. In fact, you may well find that once you know your financial abilities and limitations, you will only want those things that lie within your extended grasp. You will soon be living up to your greatest financial potential.

In the meantime, be a little realistic. Go ahead and dream about the Jaguar, but do not confuse dreams with reality. If you suddenly did come into a large sum of money, would you be better off buying a car immediately, or investing the money while you thought more about the purchase? An expensive sports car will put you in the fast lane, no doubt about that. But once you have thought about it, you just might prefer a Ford Escort or something a little more economical and less expensive. The money you invested instead of spending will soon provide you with money toward your life goals. No matter what you decide, you will have made a conscious choice.

As your personal financial plan matures, you will develop a portfolio for all seasons. You will have sufficient liquidity for cash needs, emergencies, unexpected opportunities, and investments targeted for your future and that of your family. You will have the flexibility, too, to respond to change in the money system, and you will no longer have to worry whether the economy or the income tax rules are going up or down. Come inflation, recession, or depression you will be prepared because your various investments will carry income, growth, and hedges against disaster.

An impossible dream? Not after your financial plan framework is in place. Once you have defined your goals, you will have broken through the anxiety barrier, and now you are beginning to take control. Just keep in mind that your goals are just as important as money.

THE BALANCING ACT...

Savings vs. Investing

It makes no difference whether you are just starting to invest or have been investing for many years. It is all the same. You want to feel confident about your investment decisions even if you do not think you know a lot about investing. However, it is usually a very intimidating experience. And to encourage that feeling, there are literally thousands of investment decisions to choose from, and hundreds of types of investments, with many new ones appearing on the scene each day.

You may be able to reach some of your goals just by spending more carefully and freeing up some extra money. But if you are like most people, your current income alone will not supply all the money you need. To reach most of life's major goals like buying a house or a car, funding a college education, or having a secure retirement you need to save and invest.

We hear the terms "saving" and "investing" every day. But do we ever stop to think about what they really mean? There are so many ways to save and invest. The way for you depends on many factors, such as your current financial picture, your income, the stage of life you are in, the goals you are trying to reach, and when you want to reach them.

Most of us want to put together the money we need to reach our goals as quickly as we can, but without taking risk of losing it. The key is finding the right balance between making our money work as hard as it can, without taking unnecessary risk.

What is investing? In simple terms, it means putting your money to work so you get back more than you started with.

Wouldn't it be great if you could invest your money, watch it double or triple over a short period of time, take it out when ever you wanted, and not have to worry about losing any of it?

As with any investment, there are trade-offs. Generally, those trade-offs include factors such as *RISK, RETURN and LIQUIDITY.* It is also important to understand how diversification or spreading your money among several different types of investments can help you balance your risk and reach your goals.

48

Today's investor has a great deal of choices, and many factors need to be considered in making each choice. You can choose to invest in mutual funds, stocks, bonds, certificates of deposit (CDs), collectibles, real estate, annuities, insurance policies, and... the list goes on and on. So how do you decide which investments to choose? Most investors evaluate their investments based on three factors: risk, return, and liquidity.

Risk and Return: The Balancing Act.

The risks of different investments can vary widely, but with almost everyone, there is some chance that you might not make money, and you might not even get any of your money back. In the investment world, this "chance" that you might lose some or all of your investment is called *risk*. Generally, the more risk you are willing to take in an investment, the greater chance you have of losing your money. But, for taking that risk, you usually have the opportunity for a greater reward or greater profit from your investment. In investment terms, this profit is known as *return*.

There are many types of risk involved in investing. Some types of risk are:

Financial and credit risk. This is the risk that the issuer of an investment may run into financial difficulties and not be able to honor its commitments. For example, the issuer of a bond may default or in other words, not make interest or principal payments.

Market risk. Prices in the market for various types of investments can go up or down for a wide variety of reasons that may be unrelated to the financial stability of the issuer of a particular investment. This creates risk for your investment in these markets. For example, if the stock or bond markets fall, the value of a security you own in these markets may go down.

Interest rate risk. When you invest in bonds, you run the risk that the value of your investment may go down because of changes in the general level of interest rates. In general, a rise in interest rates will cause a decline in the value of already existing bonds. Conversely, if interest rates go down, bond values go up.

Purchasing power risk. This type of risk is created by inflation, or a general rise in prices. When prices go up, the amount you can purchase for a dollar goes down. The risk associated with inflation is that your investments and the income they provide may not support your future spending requirements.

Liquidity or Ease of Access
and Its Trade-Offs

The best investment choices for you do not depend solely on how much money you need to make and how much risk you are willing to accept. Your choices also depend on when you need your money, and how quickly and easily you need to be able to convert your investment into ready cash so you can use it. This ease of access is known as *liquidity*.

If you put your money in a passbook savings account, for example, it would be liquid, or accessible. And stocks and bonds that are traded on national exchanges, such as New York Stock Exchange, often are easily bought and sold. But if you bought real estate such as an apartment building, you would have to find a buyer and sell the building to convert your investment into cash. So real property is not a very good liquid investment. Before you choose an invest-ment, it is important to understand how fast that investment can be converted into cash.

Liquid investments generally are defined as stable investments that mature in less than one year, such as bank or credit union savings and checking accounts, money market funds or accounts, short-term certificates of deposit (CDs), or treasury bills (T-bills). Since all these are easily accessible, they are liquid. Although you may have to pay a penalty for early withdrawal on a CD or receive less than you anticipated if you cash in a T-bill before maturity, that is a cost of liquidity.

In exchange for easy access and safety, your earnings (or return) on a liquid investment will be less compared to your potential earnings on less liquid or more risky investments, such as real estate. But remember, if you want safety, you usually have to give up something -- usually higher returns. And cash investments probably will not help you much toward a long-term goal, such as funding college education or saving for retirement, because inflation is likely to reduce your overall return.

Diversification: The right balance for you

As you decide where to invest your money, it is important to consider risk, return and liquidity together. High-return investments will have the greater amount of risk. Likewise, less liquid investments usually pay a higher return than those that are more liquid. However, the higher the returns, the more risk you must take.

You will want to get the returns you need to meet different goals at different times, avoid taking too much risk, and make sure some of your money is available if you need it. Generally, to meet short-term goals, you must make investments that are more liquid than those you would want for long-term goals. Generally, you can be comfortable taking more risk to meet long-term goals, since you have more time to ride out the ups and downs while seeking a greater reward down the road.

Diversification means balancing your risk by dividing your money among different types of investments -- some that are more risky, and some that are less risky. The idea is that, even if one investment loses money, another is likely to gain and overall you will come out ahead.

Look at it this way: Imagine an island with only two businesses, an umbrella stand and a suntan lotion store. When it rains, people buy umbrellas. When the sun shines, they buy suntan lotion. If you owned part of both businesses, you would make money come rain or shine.

Investing To Meet Your Goal

Now that you are familiar with some basic investment concepts, such as return, risk, liquidity, and diversification, as well as some of the investments available to you, you need to select your investments based on your goals.

Generally speaking, if your goal is short-term, such as buying a car in a year, you probably will not want to invest in stocks or mutual funds. With the ups and downs of the market, the value of your investment could go down on a short-term basis, and you might end up with less than you started with. N o r would you want to tie up your money in an Individual Retirement Account (IRA), because of the penalties for withdrawing your money before age 59.5.

On the other hand, if you do not need your money for several years, you may want to consider long-term investments that provide an opportunity for higher returns. With long-term investments, you can afford to take higher risks, since you will have years to make up for any short-term losses.

REAL ESTATE GAME
SHALL I PLAY?

At one time or another almost everyone believed that he or she would own a
home someday. But real estate has gotten
to be so expensive that the home ownership desire may not be as strong as it
once was. For most people, however, a
home still represents the most important
part of a dream, a symbol of earning
power. A house can be a measure of
success; a permanent, secure center in an
everchanging world. And it is all yours,
if you do not count the mortgage to the
bank, savings and loan, or seller financ-
ing it or in some cases the generous loan
from parents or in-laws.

Equally important, to most people,
is the fact that a house can be good
"investment." You will not find many
investments that are both practical and
financially sound, and the combination of
these elements continue to make home buying very attractive.

One of the most common questions
asked is, "Should I buy or should I
rent?" The cost of renting is far lower
than for purchase. You can usually rent

55

a home for less than what you would pay in mortgage costs and maintenance upkeep. You also would have more ready cash for investments purposes. The money you saved on the nondeductible portion of purchasing a home, such as the downpayment, the closing costs, and the taxes and maintenance would be readily available. When invested, these savings could earn money in the form of interest, dividends and other funds.

Again, the idea I am stressing is that you must determine whether you need to own your living space verses leasing your living space. Do not let the marketplace, or friends, or the media decide for you. If you feel good about the idea of owning your home but cannot explain why, then it still might be the right thing for you. If living in the "right" house is important to your career, that too can be a legitimate consideration.

Owning a home has both positive and negative points. However, if owning a home is one of your goals, you should consider applying the following steps:

1. *START SAVING FOR A DOWN PAYMENT TODAY.*

With few exceptions, you will need a down payment to get a mortgage loan. Additional cash may also be required for closing costs -- the cost to complete the purchase. You can begin your down payment fund by setting aside monthly installments from your paycheck starting now. How can you afford to save more money? Set up a spending plan, go to dinner and the movies less frequent, skip vacations and cut back on luxuries. The average first-time home buyer accumulates a down payment in just 2-1/2 years or less.

You may want to set a savings goal based on the purchase price of the home that interests you. If for example, you are looking at a home in the $150,000 range and since lenders typically require 10% to 20% of the purchase price to grant a mortgage loan, you will need to save between $15,000 to $30,000 for a down payment.

If you decide to save the down payment in 2-1/2 years, consider investing in a short-term bond fund. Although there is slightly more risk with a bond fund than with a money market fund, you might receive a higher return.

If you want to buy in less than 2-1/2 years, remember you will not have time to make up for any losses you might experience during that time from risky investments. So your best choice for this short period of time probably is safe, liquid investments, such as pass-book savings, money market accounts, or money market mutual funds. With the relatively low returns such investments offer however, you may not reach your goal in less than 2-1/2 years.

2. **FIGURE OUT THE MONTHLY PAYMENTS YOU CAN AFFORD.**

You can figure that your total monthly cost, including mortgage principal and interest, taxes, and insur-ance will be roughly 1% of an amount equal to the cost of your house, condo, or townhouse. According to many finan-cial planners, as a rule of thumb, your total monthly cost should not be more than 25% of your monthly gross income.

3. **LOOK FOR AREAS WITH DWELLINGS IN YOUR PRICE RANGE.**

If you are a first-time buyer, you may be surprised to find that new houses may be your most affordable choice. Builders often pay closing costs and offer assistance to help you purchase a new home. You may have to trade off convenience or complete privacy for affordability, however, since new houses often are located in the suburbs.

4. WATCH FOR OPPORTUNITIES THAT FIT WITHIN THE DOWN PAYMENT YOU ARE AMASSING.

Visit model homes and open houses. Watch ads in the real estate section of the paper. It may take awhile to find the right deal.

If a home has been on the market for a long time, the owner may lower the price substantially. Be one of the first to note the reduced price. Keep that down payment fund growing. Your own home gets closer and closer with each dollar you save.

5. BUY WHEN THE TIME, PRICE, DOWN PAYMENT, CLOSING COST, AND MONTHLY PAYMENT ARE RIGHT.

You may not get the house of your dreams the first time around so start buying a house or condo in your current price range. Stay in this first home 5 years or so, and you can hopefully build up some equity or dollar value in the house. If the house goes up in price, you will make a profit when you sell it. This profit, plus any salary increases and additional money you save over the 5 years, will help you move up to a better house.

The two most common types of mortgages are fixed-rate and adjustable-rate.

With a fixed-rate mortgage, your interest rate is fixed over the entire life of the loan.

With an adjustable-rate mortgage, the interest rate and your payments change periodically. The rate on adjustabable mortgages often are lower at the beginning of the term, making them attractive to purchasers who expect their salaries to increase, but need to keep their monthly payments low at the beginning.

Other types of mortgages are assumable, mortgage buy-downs, shared-equity, rollover, and balloon mortgages. These are the most common types of mortgage programs.

Historically, almost all types of real estate have been excellent hedges against inflation. For some people real estate has provided an enormous amount of money. As a matter of fact, most of the great fortunes in the United States were created by real estate investments.

Somehow we "feel" that when you own real estate, you cannot lose. However, many of us have already discovered (or will soon discover) that real estate ownership is simply not automatically profitable. The "sure thing" is no more.

Now more than ever, the key to any investment success is value. Value, of course, is the function of supply and demand. Value, has emerged as the undisputed, essential characteristic of any property. Value is value, no matter how the potential purchaser assesses it - - by conducting an indepth computer analysis or by simply stepping back from the property and asking, "How do I feel about this property?"

There is no shortage of opportunities in real estate, but that could be said for a number of other investments. The difference about real estate is the time it takes to invest and the time you should expect to hold it.

Let me emphasize again that the vast majority of people who have made sizeable profits through investing in real estate were conservative people investing for the long term. They were not looking for a killing over night. Many of them just happen to be in the right place at the right time.

Over the years I have learned that when investing, you must have a lot of patience as well staying power. Mistakes in real estate can be especially disastrous because of the large amount of money usually involved. If you can afford to hold on, you will find that things more often than not turn around in

your favor. Many investors, even successful ones, at times must sell their hold-
ings because they are so heavily in debt
(overleveraged) they cannot weather the
bad times any other way.

Real estate, almost more than any
other investment, can be characterized by
leverage. That is, borrowing money to
buy what you want with as little cash as
possible out of pocket. Unless there is
a tax change, the great advantage to
investing in real estate is that you can
deduct more than the amount invested
without being liable to pay off the
leverage.

The deductions can help you create
tax losses to shelter income from other
sources. Leverage is the important
factor in creating these losses, which
come about, for example, because depreciation is based on the gross purchase
price and interest is charged against the
amount you owe. Your paper loss from
depreciation may be greater than your
payments, and the loss you finally
calculate will probably be much greater
than your initial cash investment. The
more leverage used, the greater the paper
loss and the better the opportunity for
capital appreciation or real loss.

These are uncertain times, and I
believe that real estate investors may be
poised at the edge of a no-win situation.

People have grown to expect quick appreciation from real estate, and if it does not happen, the market could become depressed. Today, with the higher risk associated with increased real estate uncertainty, portfolio diversification also becomes an even more important factor.

If you have some cash to risk and you find real estate appealing, you have two fundamental decisions to make. The first concerns your portfolio. What portions of your discretionary income and savings should be invested in real property. The second is whether you wish to be a landlord or to invest in group ownership with professional management.

You have to come to grips with the idea of being a landlord. Do you want to be bothered with leaking roofs, plumbing problems, heating and air conditioner problems, dishwasher leaking, and so on and so on. Owning rental property is like owning a second business, very time consuming.

Another possibility is to create a joint venture with one or more other investors. This alternative also requires a substantial amount of funds and limits your diversification. Initially it is just as much work. You still need to research, evaluate, and negotiate, and then someone has to manage it.

63

I believe that just about everyone should have some real estate in his or her portfolio. Even if you are retired, you can select conservative real estate investments that will produce good income with low amounts of debt.

THE FUTURE...
401K, IRA, KEOGH, THRIFT PLANS

Planning for retirement does not mean you must actually plan to retire. It simply ensures that the money you do not need now to live on will pay good dividends when you are ready to retire.

What you invest today will help replace the money you will not be earning if you want to slow down or in fact retire. Ultimately, the primary goal of retirement planning is a stable, income-producing investment fund that will enable you to maintain your current or near current standard of living.

In the mist of the 1990's with companies in the down sizing mode, it is to your advantage to do planning for the possibility of early retirement with lump sum pay out. By pre-planning, you will have given careful consideration to how those funds will be utilized to maximize your future return.

Unfortantly, a large percentage of our population approach retirement years with no preparation for retirement thereby looking totally to social security and a very small retirement fund for their total retirement income. In most cases this income will not provide the funds needed to cover our steady inflation rate of housing, food, and all the other necessities.

I believe that there is a strong possibility that by the time the baby-boomers are ready to retire there just might not be social socurity funds available. Our population as a whole is living longer, thereby requiring more funds to support the retired. While at the same time the employment rate is down so less funds are being put into the retirement system and at the same time more funds are going out of the system. The end result is that our system will run out of money, therefore, if you have not planned for your retirement, you will not have sufficient retirement funds to maintain your previous lifestyle.

Now, this is just my opinion. Government has recognized the need for adequate retirement planning, therefore, it has provided tax incentives to encourage individuals to do some of their own planning for the future. Another way of putting it is, if you do not plan for yourself, then you are on your own.

INDIVIDUAL RETIREMENT ACT
(IRA)

Thanks to the Economic Recovery Tax Act of 1981, anyone who earns compensation may open an Individual Retirement Account.

It appears that people who have not invested in IRA's are making a big mistake, at least that's what the government and institutions with a vested interest would have you believe.

Our circumstances dictate our action. The question is not whether you want to save, but are you able to save at this time.

Do not be fooled by all the hype. It really does not matter whether you use a bank, savings and loan, mutual funds or some other type of IRA investment. The main focus is on starting a portfolio that includes a number of investments to maximize your return during the retirement years.

Many people think of IRA's simply as a retirement savings account. In fact, an IRA is an investment that provides tax advantages that may vary depending on your situation. A single individual can invest up to $2,000 per year. If you are married and both you and your spouse work, you could each invest up to $2,000 per year. If your spouse does not work, together you can invest up to $2,250 per year, as long as no more that $2,000 is invested in either your account or your spouse's account. If you are covered by an employer's retirement plan some or none of the IRA maybe deductible. For example, if you are single and your adjusted gross income is over $35,000, none of the contribution is deductible.

The interest earned on an IRA is not taxable until those funds are distributed to you. So your money can grow faster than it would if you had to pay taxes each year on the earnings. The potential tax deductions and tax-deferred growth associated with IRA's are attractive, but there are some drawbacks. If you withdraw funds from an IRA before your retirement, the withdrawal is taxable at a higher rate and may be subject to an additional Federal tax penalty.

401(k)
A DEFERRED PLAN

The 401(k) is one of many qualified plans that can be set up by an employer for the benefit of employees. It allows employees to build up savings, which are paid out at retirement or on termination of employment. The employees pay taxes on this money only when they draw it out, usually at retirement; until such time, the funds accumulate tax deferred. The main feature of the 401(k) plan is that employees can shift a great deal of their income tax liability to a later date. Funds set aside in a 401(k) plan are considered "deferred compensation" and are not reported to the IRS as income. The income on the amount set aside is not taxable until the tax year the taxpayer withdraws the funds. You can have a 401(k) and IRA at the same time.

This is considered a profit-sharing plan, an agreement between a corporation and its employees that allows the employees to share in company profits. Because of this, there are complex requirements. Whether you are highly paid or not so highly paid, if your employer offers one of these plans you will almost certainly want to channel into it all the retirement savings you can. Not only can you place more money in a 401(k) than in an IRA, but your company may match a portion of your contributions. In addition to your being able to borrow against this plan, many of the rules involving the withdrawal of funds from the 401(k) are more favorable than those an IRA.

A KEOGH PLAN

If you are self-employed or in a partnership, you can set up a Keogh Plan, which is a tax-deferred pension plan. You may contribute to both a Keogh and IRA. Though similar, because both allow you to deduct your contributions and in both the investments grow tax deferred, you can contribute more to the Keogh than you can to the IRA.

If you are thinking about setting up a Keogh for your unincorporated business, hire someone else to worry about the details. Consult with your accountant for explanations on how things apply to you.

THRIFT PLAN
COMPANY SPONSORED

Your employer may offer a thrift plan, sometimes called a savings plan or savings incentive plan. A thrift plan invites you to make contributions, if you wish, of a portion of your salary usually about 2% to 5% of your gross wages, but sometimes more. The employer is committed to match your contributions, usually up to 5% of your gross.

Some plans allow you to contribute unmatched dollars once you exceed the employer's maximum matching level. All of which is tax deferred. You can also borrow against your funds for emergencies, school, real estate, and a few other reasons.

ACKNOWLEDGMENTS

To adequately recognize and thank all those who provided assistance and encouragement during the writing of this book would be a difficult task. But to some of those special people who clearly influenced my thinking or provided me with substantial encouragement and technical assistance, I offer my sincere gratitude.

Stephanie Stone, a consultant and professional writer as well as a good friend, suggested the name of my book. While knowing little about financial planning, nonetheless she spent many hours acting as a sounding board and providing truly valuable assistance in the writing of this book. She has used information from the book and now her financial future is much brighter.

Francine Autry-Scott, writer and publisher, stated that the book is an excellent resource of information for the person aspiring to achieve greater financial success. It gives practical advise on how to make your money work for you, regardless of one's financial status.

Thomas Logan, co-worker and financial analyst for the Department of Justice. After reviewing the book, Thomas has now implemented a number of the recommendations for cutting expenses and creating additional cash flow.

Robin Waller, ex-banker, financier, currently a financial planner for Nisson Corp., and very astute business woman, provided additional feedback from a banker's point of view. She made sure that the financial information was simple enough to be understood and used by all.

Ruth Mills, retired English teacher and editor of my book, evaluated and offered constructive criticism in the course of reviewing my book. Her very first comment was pertaining to a dangling participle. One word that best describes her...quality.

----------BOOK ORDER FORM----------

Warren Publishing Company
P.O. Box 146
Pomona, CA 91769
(909) 465-9733

$_____ Subtotal of books($9.95
           each)

+-------- Shipping and Handling
           ($1.30 per item)

+-------- Tax (California residents
           add 8.25%)

$_____ Total

Send check or money order (no cash
or C.O.D's)

Name_____

Address_____

City_____State_____

Zip Code_____

Please allow 2 weeks for delivery